The Irish Home Buyer's Guide to Snagging

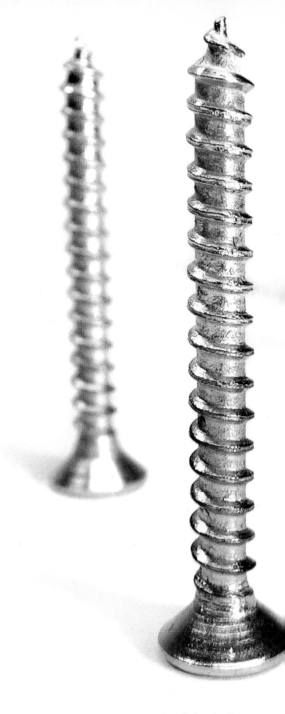

Published by Liberties Practical, an imprint of Liberties Press
Guinness Enterprise Centre, Taylor's Lane, Dublin 8, Ireland.
www.LibertiesPress.com TEL: +353 (1) 415 1224
Editors: Michael Freeman and Liberties Press
Design: www.designforlife.ie
Printing: Colour Books
ISBN 10: 1-905483-13-9
ISBN 13: 978-1-905483-13-6
Trade enquiries to CMD Distribution

Acknowledgements

I wish to place on record my thanks to the many people
who contributed towards the production of this guide.

I thank my wife Trish who helped me with the
research, writing and production.

I thank the many people who gave willingly and frankly of
their comments and appraisals of the original manuscript.

I thank you the reader for your attention and for buying
this guide. I hope that the tips and pointers help you to
confidently approach your snag list, one of the final
hurdles in acquiring the property of your dreams.

- John Boyle

John Boyle

During his career in the USA, the UK and his native Ireland, John Boyle has helped thousands of home buyers to satisfactorily complete their Snag Lists.

He is a native of Co. Mayo where he attended St. Colman's College, Claremorris. He attended the Regional Technical College, Sligo and graduated from the Dublin Institute of Technology from which he holds a City and Guilds Certificate in Carpentry and Joinery Craft.

Every day in his working life as a site manager and finishing foreman for one of Ireland's leading construction companies, he interacts with builders, construction staff, developers, decorators, designers, solicitors, architects, surveyors, professional snaggers, amateur snaggers, DIY snaggers and homeowners to ensure that property is finished to the highest standard.

John Boyle's experience includes the restoration and renovation of single family homes, construction of large shopping centres, supervision of large commercial projects with clients including Sony, IBM and GPA in the US, and working as project manager with a top New York interior designer on private residential and commercial retail spaces.

Whether you are a homebuyer, a seller, an architect, builder, surveyor, lawyer, estate agent, or know nothing about snagging you will benefit from John Boyle's advice in this unique guide.

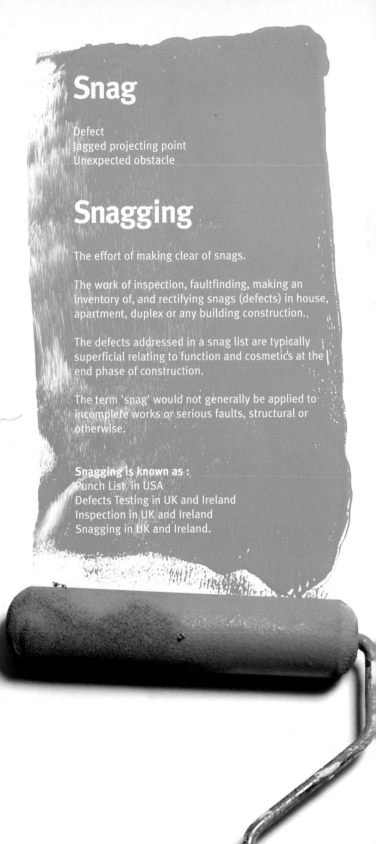

Snag

Defect
Jagged projecting point
Unexpected obstacle

Snagging

The effort of making clear of snags.

The work of inspection, faultfinding, making an
inventory of, and rectifying snags (defects) in house,
apartment, duplex or any building construction.

The defects addressed in a snag list are typically
superficial relating to function and cosmetics at the
end phase of construction.

The term 'snag' would not generally be applied to
incomplete works or serious faults, structural or
otherwise.

Snagging is known as :
Punch List in USA
Defects Testing in UK and Ireland
Inspection in UK and Ireland
Snagging in UK and Ireland.

Contents

It's **Your Move**

You're Moving! You're Selling!
You're Buying! You're Investing!
You're Renovating!

Moving to a new home, selling your present one, or buying or 'cheering up' an old house or property investment is exciting.

While it may take time and money, and you may experience the entire scale of emotions ranging from despair to utter bliss, it can be immensely rewarding.

The Irish Home Buyer's Guide to Snagging will help you to make the most of your move, or your buying or investment decision. Whether it's your first time to buy, invest or move, and whether you're a novice or an experienced snagger, you'll benefit.

By following the advice in this guide, you can identify inevitable problems that occur in house building and you can save many days of your time and hundreds if not thousands of euro.

It shows you how to carry out a comprehensive snag list from the interior to the exterior and from top to bottom of your house or property.

The numerous hints and tips should help you to actually add value to your new property.

To ensure that you can complete a comprehensive snag list, the guide includes a specially designed Universal Snag List, which you can adapt to fault test any property.

"The guide also shows you how to identify a suitable property and how to use the expertise of your estate agent, architect or surveyor."

Your **Professional Team**

Your Estate Agent

A visit to an estate agent is usually the first call for people thinking of buying, selling, renting or investing in property.

The estate agent works like a broker bringing builders/developers, buyers and sellers into the marketplace and liaises with solicitors (see below) and financial institutions (see below) where necessary.

Before you go to the estate agent, you can do some preliminary research. Read the property section of newspapers and any property magazines or e-zines related to your search. Log on to the Internet and, for example, key in the word 'property' or 'estate agent' and your location e.g. the county or town or village in which you are interested into your Altavista, Dogpile, Go, Google, Excite, Hotbot, Lycos, Meta Crawler, Yahoo or other search engine.

Once you have identified a number of properties that suit your objective, the location you seek, your dream, and your pocket, the estate agent will organise for you to visit them.

The estate agent will tell you the asking price for the property, although this price may be lower or higher than advertised.

If you wish you can make an offer, which should be the amount that you consider that the property is worth, and what you can afford.

The estate agent will advise you whether the client is interested in your offer.

If you don't buy, no hard feelings, there's always another day and possibly another property not far away and the estate agent will be delighted to see you again.

If you decide to buy, you will be asked to confirm this by paying a booking deposit in your name.

Contact your solicitor immediately and make an appointment to sign the contracts (see solicitor). This will be accompanied by the remainder of the deposit which is often 10% of the purchase price.

A buyer does not generally pay a fee to the estate agent. As the buyer you may, depending on the value or size of the house, have to pay a tax called Stamp Duty to the Revenue Commissioners.

As a buyer, you may have to pay a tax to the Revenue called Stamp Duty. Above certain values of property, it could amount to between 3% and 9% of the value of the property.

The amount or rate of Stamp Duty that you have to pay on the purchase of a residential property, whether it is a house or an apartment, will depend on whether you are a first time buyer, an owner occupier, or an investor and whether you satisfy certain conditions within those categories.

For example, if you are a first time buyer, and the property is below 125 sq. metres in area, you may be exempt from Stamp Duty subject to certain clawback conditions. Check with your financial adviser, tax adviser, solicitor or estate agent. See also the website: www. revenue. ie

The price of your house is usually set by a qualified professional valuer who is generally a member of the estate agent's staff. When a mortgage or loan is being evaluated, the property is usually assessed by a valuer appointed by the bank or building society or independent valuer.

If you are selling your home, the estate agent will meet with you, assess your home for market value, arrange advertising, arrange appointment times for viewings, liaise with your solicitor for the signing of contracts and generally ease you through the selling process.

For the services of the estate agent, a seller pays advertising costs, fees and the estate agent's commission.

A number of estate agents specialise in rental properties. They find tenants, arrange leases and manage properties as a service to the property owner.

Your Solicitor

Your solicitor will play an integral role in the process of transferring ownership of your new property to you. The complex legal work involved in property transactions is called conveyancing.

All property transactions are complex and are subject to the law of the land and to the rules, regulations and by-laws of the Local Authority or County Council.

Whether you are about to engage an architect to build a one-off property to your specifications, are planning to purchase a second-hand property, or have identified a property in a development "off the plans", it is important to make immediate contact with your solicitor. This will ensure that you understand what must be done to ensure that the legal and also financial process runs smoothly.

Suggested topics for discussion include: Legal fees (usually a percentage of the cost of the property), an explanation of the legal requirements, duration of the legal process, and what documentation will be required from you.

Remember that three solicitors may be involved in the whole transaction:
- Your own solicitor
- The financial institution's solicitor
- The builder/developer's solicitor

Your Financial Institution

Financing for the cost of a property may come from any number of sources e.g. funds from the sale of a previous property, gifts, savings, SSIA or even winnings from the National Lottery.

However, most people purchasing a property will use a financial institution such as a bank, building society, credit union or mortgage adviser/broker. Some builder/developers may offer finance through a particular financial institution.

A mortgage is a loan backed by the value of a property. Because property

has proven to be a safe bet over at least a hundred years, mortgages are offered at interest rates that are much lower than for ordinary loans.

Don't be afraid to shop around for the best deal. You may not fit the customer profile that some banks or building societies are looking for, or they may not fit your requirements.

To get the most from your financial institution, contact your branch and seek a meeting with the manager advising that you are looking for a mortgage. Ask about the pros and cons of fixed versus variable rate mortgages, endowment mortgages, and interest-only mortgages. Ask also about what documentation you will be required to submit, e.g. P6o, or business/company accounts.

Your Builder/Developer

Your builder/developer constructs the property you are about to purchase. Depending on whether it's a one-off house or a part of a larger development, the amount of contact you will have with the builder/developer will vary.

Ask the Companies Office if the builder/developer is registered and if his/her company returns are up to date. This is especially important if you are purchasing a one-off property.

Visit other developments that have been completed by the same builder/developer. Ask previous customers what their impressions are and if they have been satisfied with his/her work.

If you think you will want to make changes to the planned property, contact your builder as soon as possible.

Vital **Decisions**

Sit down with a pen and sheet of paper. On the paper write the answer to the most powerful question of all - WHY?

Why are you planning to move house, sell, buy, renovate?

YOUR REASON WHY MAY BE ONE OR A COMBINATION OF REASONS:

Aesthetics -   A more beautiful area, well designed, Victorian, Edwardian, Modern, Contemporary, Minimalist and so on

Environment - Less pollution, cleaner air, more countryside

Social - Where friends are, where crime is lower, where children can mix easily

Cultural - A better area for quality of life

Political - Tired of the present neighbours

Lifestyle - Closer to the gym, the swimming pool, the golf course

Life Cycle - Slimming down, preparing a nest egg for the next phase

Work Convenient - Closer to work, cut costs of travel - time and money

Business Convenient - Closer to clients

Family Convenient - Closer to the child-minder, close to the créche

Amenities - Closer to the playground, the football/hurling pitch

Facilities - Closer to shops, schools, sportsground, bus, church, pub, community centre, night clubs.

Economic - Opportunity to buy where value of property will increase more and faster, need bigger or smaller house or apartment, need an investment, make good use of money to buy an apartment in the city rather than pay rent for a student going to college and so on.

If you want to live near your work, buying a house close by can cut your costs, extend the life of your car and leave you more time to indulge in your family, your favourite sports and so on.

If your objective is to buy to sell, make sure that you check out the implications of Capital Gains Tax and other costs beforehand. Meanwhile, this guide will help you to add value to your house in order to sell at a premium price.

If you are planning to invest, it may be better to invest in a property in a run-down area, and 'do it up'. Use this guide to help you. You may, when house prices increase faster, sell it and make a profit that will allow you to move to a bigger house or make a different investment.

If your objective is to buy to keep, use the Irish Home Buyer's Guide to Snagging to keep your home ship shape and up to date. Use it to guide your spring cleaning every year.

Whatever your objective or goal, use the Irish Home Buyer's Guide to Snagging to check ongoing maintenance and as the ultimate health check for what is probably your biggest and most important investment.

Zoned for Development - Go to the County Council or Local Authority planning office and check what the surrounding area is zoned for and any developments planned at present or in the near future. If you are on good terms with a local builder or developer or estate agent, he or she may tell you what the real story is.

Why **Snag?**

You have arranged your finance with the building society or the bank. You have cleared the legal and conveyancing matters with your solicitor. Now you are about to engage your builder to build or renovate your new home, second-hand house, duplex, or apartment.

If you are about to make a property decision, you are about to make one of the biggest investments of your life. You may of course be quite wealthy and be investing in a second or third house. You have the assurance that such investment has proven to date to be both safe and wise over the long term. Congratulations on your decision.

Your house may be a home or an investment. Or, it may be both a home and an investment. Whether it is small, big or vast, it should be snagged.

Snagging is the practice of checking that your new home or investment has been built and completed according to your contract specifications, and that all minor defects have been highlighted and addressed.

A snag list is the vital checklist, inventory or faultfinder that you and your builder complete to ensure that your new home or investment has been completed to the highest standards. All good builders welcome and encourage you to submit your snag list so that they may rectify any problems to your mutual satisfaction.

A comprehensive snag list will highlight faults, defects and pitfalls that can be remedied before you buy your house. In addition, it will ensure that you have identified the cosmetic problems that even the best-intentioned builders and developers miss or overlook.

Architects, builders, surveyors and estate agents will tell you that snagging is mainly about cosmetics. A good snag list can lead to a property being finished to a higher standard than it otherwise might have been. A better cosmetic finish could ultimately add between 10% and 20% to your property's value. It can add value to your house, cut costs and ensure that you have peace of mind.

Make sure that you have snagged your property before your builder leaves your site ("and your sight") forever. We recommend that you have the snag list completed before payment is finalised and before you move in.

Builders, solicitors, building societies and banks recommend that you do a comprehensive snag list. Our Universal Snag List given within this guide is comprehensive.

You may engage an architect, surveyor, engineer, or building professional to carry out the snag list for you while also using this guide. Or, using this guide, you may confidently do it all yourself.

The **Snagging Process**

Your first objective is to ensure that the Builder/Developer has fulfilled the contract with you in building or renovating your house or apartment.

If the contract has not been fulfilled, you should ensure that any problems, faults or defects are rectified to your satisfaction.

Your second objective is to capitalise on the contacts of the builder/developer while on site to facilitate any extras you may require.

Builders and developers are only human and respond to reason. We suggest that your builder/developer can be your best friend if you treat him/her with respect. Unreasonable attacks are most often counter productive.

Good builders will build according to standard building regulations and you can be assured that the structure of the building will be sound if you engage a builder/developer who is registered with the Construction Industry Federation and who is registered with HomeBond, Premier or others. For added peace of mind, ask the builder or architect to confirm that the building complies with the most up-to-date building regulations, including, but not limited to Part L and Part M of the Building Regulations.

Excellent builders/developers strive to exceed the standard regulations and you will get quality in excess of your expectations and perhaps your technical knowledge. Do remember that a lot of the construction process is done by hand and a uniform factory finish is not always possible.

The structure will be sound and the only outstanding matters will be cosmetic.

These cosmetic matters may include defects in painting, or plastering, doors that don't close well, scrapes on glass and so on. These will be identified when doing the snag list and should be rectified to everybody's satisfaction before finalising the sale agreement.

Snagging Equipment

To complete your snag list quickly and effectively, you need some basic snagging equipment. Here is a checklist:

1. Universal Snag List included with this guide

2. Step ladder

3. Torch

4. Notepad

5. Pen and pencil

6. Measuring tape (Measuring while snagging can be useful for the subsequent tasks of ordering curtains, blinds, carpeting and/or other floor covering)

7. Hairdryer for checking sockets

8. Screwdrivers (Philips and flathead)

9. In certain cases, the snagger will need a hard hat, good protective boots and a high visibility vest.
The builder should advise if this is necessary

10. Mobile phone - to contact builder to provide access to the property. Remember to phone the builder for access.

11. Spirit level

12. Light bulbs - 60 watt. (for checking if light fixtures work).

Common **Snag Points**

To get you into the frame of mind before you go snagging, here are some common snag points:

- Doors that do not hang properly
- Uneven floors
- Scratched window panes
- Kitchen units out of kilter
- Bathroom fittings that fail to work
- Cracks in ceilings and walls
- Faulty electrics
- Dampness on walls
- Dampness around window sills
- Poorly finished plastering
- Cracked Tiles
- Dampness in the attic
- Missing Roof tiles
- Broken Fencing

Interior Snagging

Start on the inside. Turn on the heating to allow the radiators to heat up. In each room, fix a starting point, move clockwise and finish at that starting point. Indicate this on the snag list for your builder.

In every room inspect walls and ceilings, windows, doors, floor, fireplace, skirting and architraves, plumbing, electrics, paintwork, ventilation and fire prevention.

Starting, say in the kitchen, first look at ceilings and follow by scanning the floors. Having completed the inspection of the kitchen move onto the bathroom and so on.

Once you have completed your snag list, your builder can address any problems identified.

KITCHEN

LOOK FOR
KITCHEN PRESSES / COUNTERTOPS / SINK AND APPLIANCES

TAKE ACTION

Kitchen presses - All doors should be hung straight. There should be consistent gaps between adjacent doors and drawer fronts.

Looking along the line of the kitchen units, you should see that they all line up. Check that all handles or knobs are present and are installed neatly. Check all doors and drawers for ease of opening. Ensure that there are no paint splashes on kitchen units, or scratches on surface.

Check the interior of kitchen units. Screws attaching the units to the wall should be covered by plastic caps. Take a close look under the sink. The back of this unit will have been removed for plumbing. Check that it has been reinstalled securely and neatly. The middle shelf of this unit will have been cut out for the waste pipe from the sink. Ensure that this has been done neatly. (See Plumbing p.33)

All units should be clean and Joints between sections of wood should be tight and neatly finished.

Countertops - Check your contract to ensure that the countertop provided is as specified. The most common countertops are made of Formica or granite. Check for scratches. The edge of the countertop closest to the wall should be sealed with a thin line of silicone. (See photo)

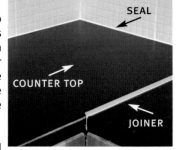

KITCHEN COUNTER

Sink and appliances - The sink should be securely fastened - you should not be able to move it. It should be sealed to the countertop - check this by running your fingernail around the under surface of the sink edge. It should be tight and almost impossible to insert your fingernail. Check the sink for scratches. Run water and check under the sink to see that the waste pipe is not leaking.

If appliances are not supplied, measure openings provided to ensure that they meet your needs (see Technical Tips p.56). There should be a hole, 100mm in diameter, in an exterior wall for the extractor fan hose. This should be in close proximity to the site for the extractor fan, and should not be covered by kitchen presses.

If you have chosen to install a stainless steel extractor, the location for the vent is critical. You must inform your builder in the very early stages. Where appliances are not supplied check that the sockets are appropriately positioned. Where appliances are supplied, check that they work and that they are not scratched or damaged. You should be furnished with the warranty and instruction manual for each appliance by the builder, typically at time of closing.

WALLS AND CEILINGS

LOOK FOR
CORRECT ALIGNMENT / PLASTERING FINISH /
POPPED NAILS / CRACKS

CEILING, COVING, WALL

TAKE ACTION

Correct alignment - To check that walls are "plumb" i.e. perpendicular with the floor, look at the top and bottom edges of a doorframe. The horizontal distance from the top of the doorframe to the nearest corner, and from the bottom of the doorframe to the nearest corner, should be the same.

If you suspect that the wall may not be plumb, test with a spirit level.

Plastering finish - It is important to remember that plastering is done by hand and that therefore a completely uniform "factory" finish is not possible. However, noticeable joints, where sheets of plasterboard meet underneath the plastering, should not be visible. Trowel marks, indentations, bulges, or lines, should not be visible either.

Popped nails - If the plaster falls off the head of an underlying nail, it is called a 'popped nail'. When noting this on your snag list, request that the

builder inserts a screw above or below the offending nail. The offending nail should then be tapped in, the plaster filled and the area repainted. This approach will prevent recurrence.

POPPED NAIL

Cracks - Minor hairline cracks are caused by the drying-out process and are common. These should be raked out and re-plastered. However, more extensive cracks could indicate structural problems. Bring this to the attention of your builder, and if in doubt, seek independent professional advice.

*"**Minor hairline cracks are caused** by the drying-out process and are common. They should be raked out and re-plastered"*

WINDOWS

Windows may be PVC, aluminum, timber, softwood or hardwood. Each type of window can present similar problems.

LOOK FOR

CHIPS ON FRAME / SCRAPES ON FRAME / HINGES / LOCKS AND HANDLES / SCRATCHES ON GLASS / SEALANT / WINDOW BOARD

TAKE ACTION

Chips on frame - Most minor chips on PVC and timber windows can be patched. Note them on your snag list.

Scrapes on frame - Most scrapes on window frames can be sanded and filled.

Hinges - Check that the main window opens 90 degrees and moves with ease. Make sure that the track on the bottom of the window frame is clean.

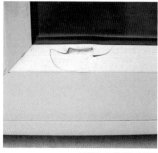

CHIP ON FRAME

Locks and handles - Always check handles for ease of opening. Depending on fire regulations, some handles have locks. Check that keys fit and turn.

Scratches on glass - Stand two metres back from the glass and check glass for scratches. Do this in sunlight if possible.

Sealant - This is the seal that weatherproofs between the glass and frame. Check that it is continuous, even, and neatly joined. If there is fogging of the window pane which can't be wiped off, the double glazing seal is faulty.

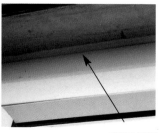

SEALANT

Window board - This is a ledge at the bottom of the interior window. It may be constructed of timber, PVC or plasterboard. Check to see that it is level. This is usually apparent. To confirm, measure from floor level to each end of the window board and compare, or use a spirit level. The edge of the board should protrude in past the surrounding wall, and extend past the edges of the window equally on both sides. If the window frame is made of timber, check for popped nails (see Popped Nails p.24). Timber and plasterboard will be painted. Timber may also be varnished. These surfaces should be snagged accordingly. (See Paintwork p.35)

DOORS

LOOK FOR

FINISH / WARPING / CHIPS AND SCRATCHES / LOCKS, HANDLES AND HINGES / EASE OF MOTION / DOOR CLOSERS / FIRE STRIP

TAKE ACTION

Finish - Most interior doors are wooden, and may be painted or varnished. Ensure that the finish is even. Check that the paint/varnish has not formed drops or that it has not run onto hardware such as hinges or handles. For interior PVC doors, e.g. sliding patio doors, check the interior rubber seal on the glass. This may have been damaged during window cleaning and if so should be replaced.

DAMAGED DOOR FRAME

Warping - Warping occurs when the wood becomes distorted, causing the door to twist slightly. This may be indicated if the door does not close properly. With the door in a closed position, its edge should line up with the frame with an approximately three mm gap all the way around.

Chips and scratches - Check the surface of doors for chips and scratches. The bottom edge of the door is particularly prone to chips where it may have been jammed in the open position during construction. Again remember to check glass panels in doors for scratches.

Locks, Handles and Hinges - (Hardware). Close the door, ensuring that the latch catches in the receiver in the doorframe.

With the latch still engaged, attempt to open the door - if the lock has been properly installed this should not be possible. Turn the key to see if the lock (deadbolt) fits into the receiver. Check that the key can lock both sides of the door.

With the door open, look into the receiver opening. The aperture should be smooth and well finished.

LOCK RECEIVER

Check the handle for ease of motion. Hinges may be made of steel or brass. Steel is usually painted and should be snagged as for all paintwork. Brass and all other hardware should be free of paint and scratches.

All pre-drilled holes in hinges should have screws. Ensure that the cutout sections for hinges on doors and frames are even, smooth and that no excess gaps are present.

Ease of Motion - The door should move smoothly throughout its full arc. When stopped in the open position, it should stay put and not move further of its own accord. (exception - see Door Closers below)

Door Closers - In certain circumstances due to fire regulations, interior doors in apartments will be fitted with door closers. These devices cause the door to close automatically. They may be concealed (built into the door and frame) or surface mounted. To check correct function, open the door to 90 degrees. The door should close and the latch engage.

Fire Strip - The amount of fire protection on interior doors is determined by the Fire Safety regulations and the Fire Officer's requirements are communicated to the architect at the time of planning. The architect, as part of the closing process, will produce a certificate of compliance to confirm that the regulations have been adhered to. Your solicitor will incorporate the certificate into your closing documentation.

Depending on the size and design of the development, a fire strip may not be required at all, or it may be present in different amounts. If present, it is a narrow strip along the centre of the door edge and/or the centre of the doorframe.

Check that it has not been damaged. Occasionally, it may have been removed. If so, this will be apparent by the presence of a narrow channel along the surface which should have contained it.

FLOORS

LOOK FOR
TYPE OF FLOOR / FINISH / LEVEL SURFACE / DEBRIS

TAKE ACTION

Type of floor - The floor provided should be as specified in your contract. Many houses and townhouses are completed with plywood, chipboard or

floorboards upstairs, and concrete floor slabs downstairs. One - off houses may have sand and cement screed floors. Apartment floors are usually finished in concrete floor slabs. However, this will vary from area to area and builder to builder, so check your contract.

GAP BETWEEN FLOORBOARDS AND SKIRTING

Finish - Be aware of the difference between floorboard and finished timber floors. When floorboards have been installed, they are not intended as a finished floor surface, and will not have been sanded or varnished. Snagging should be carried out with this in mind. A finished timber floor however, be it solid, semisolid or laminate, will have a finished surface.

All floor boards, including plywood and chipboard, should be securely fastened down. No holes or tripping hazards should be present. Check thoroughly around radiators as floors may have been removed for access during checking of heating systems and may not have been reinstalled neatly. Joints between wood segments should generally be tight.

Snagging for a concrete floor is the same as that for sand and cement screed. The floor should have a smooth finish without bumps and hollows. Observe the surface for cracks. Minor cracks may occur as part of the drying out process, and can be addressed by the builder by raking out and filling the crack. More substantial cracks in the floor are a cause for concern as they may indicate structural problems. Bring this to the attention of the builder. But if in any doubt, or if there is any disagreement, seek independent professional advice.

Where there is an apartment below yours, a soundproof membrane should be installed on top of the finished concrete. This is usually made of cork. Ensure that the surface is continuous and without any tears. Joints between cork segments should be tight. The cork membrane should be attached to the concrete by a coating of glue and it should not be possible to lift it at any point.

"The floor should have a smooth
finish, without bumps and hollows"

Level surface - The gap between the skirting and floor surface should be minimal and consistent. If there is a much larger gap at any point it may indicate that the floor is off level. This may be indicated also if a door catches against the floor in the open position. You can confirm this by using a spirit level. Ask the builder to investigate and correct.

Where concrete floors are off level, corrective action may be taken by applying a levelling compound. If your plan is to subsequently install a wood floor or tiles, it is essential that the underlying floor is level.

Debris - All floors should be free of debris.

FIREPLACES

LOOK FOR
FINISH / SOLID FUEL OR GAS

TAKE ACTION
Finish - There are many types of fireplace on the market. The fireplace supplied should be similar to that in the show house, or as agreed with the builder on a client by client basis.

TYPICAL FIREPLACE

Ensure that it is clean and scratch free and ensure that the fireplace surround is sealed to the wall - no gaps should be visible. To check if it is level, use a spirit level on the hearth.

Check behind the fireback by putting your hand up the chimney. You should not be able to feel any gap behind the fireback.

FIREPLACE MEETS WALL

Solid fuel or Gas - The hearths for solid fuel or gas fireplaces are different in construction. Gas fireplaces are commonly supplied as standard in the Dublin area.

If you have chosen to have a solid fuel fireplace, this must be communicated to the builder as soon as possible. In this case, expansion joints should be apparent at the back of the hearth near the grate.

If it is a gas fireplace, a 6mm copper pipe will be visible at the back of the grate for a gas connection. The opening where the gas supply pipe emerges from the wall must be neatly finished. On one side of the fireplace there will be a gas turnoff switch - a 100 mm square plastic plate with a circular hole in the centre- for turning gas supply on/off.

"The floor of the attic,
including the top surface of the attic door, should be insulated"

ATTIC SPACE

Attic spaces are not usually finished with a solid floor and are left with joists exposed. Joists are timbers running parallel on the floor of the attic at intervals. Spaces between joists are filled with insulation. When inspecting the attic, walk only on joists for safety reasons.

LOOK FOR
CLEAR ACCESS / INSULATION / FELT /
ADEQUATE VENTILATION / SECURE TIMBERWORK / PARTY WALL

ATTIC

TAKE ACTION

Clear access - The access to an attic is usually from the upstairs landing. It should be possible to place a ladder on the landing clear of the stairs with enough space to ensure safety. There should be no cables, pipes or timbers crossing over the opening to the attic.

Insulation - The floor of the attic, including the top surface of the attic door, should be insulated. Insulation should extend to the sides and top of the water tank, but not the underside. This allows the heat of the house to prevent the water tank from freezing in cold weather. All water pipes should be lagged (insulated).

Felt - This is a membrane between the rafters and the tile or slate. In older houses, check to see if this is present, as it would be very costly to install later, necessitating removal of the tiles/slates. Felt should be laid neatly across the rafters and joints should overlap. The felt should not sag downwards between rafters.

Adequate ventilation - see Ventilation p.36

Secure timberwork - Shake each timber to ensure that it is securely fastened and held in place.

Party wall - This is the dividing wall between two properties. In the attic, it should extend fully to the underside of the felt lining of the roof tiles. This is for fire prevention and also to limit sound transmission. No roof timbers should penetrate this wall.

Note: An attic light is generally not included. It is advisable to request one as an extra. Request that the switch be positioned near the attic door.

Note: Ask the builder, if possible, to provide a few floorboards for the attic. This will transform the attic into a convenient storage place.

SKIRTING AND ARCHITRAVES

Skirting: A narrow board along the base of an interior wall.
Architrave: A moulded frame around a doorway or window.

LOOK FOR
JOINTS / FINISH / LEVEL

TAKE ACTION

Joints - Joints in the timberwork occur at corners, or along straight sections where two pieces of timber had to be used. In general there should be few joints along straight sections - full lengths of timber should be used where possible.

Where there is a joint along a straight surface of a wall, the joint should be cut at a 45 degree angle (mitred). It should not be cut end to end. At architrave corners, joints should also be mitred.

MITRED JOINT
AT SKIRTING

At room corners, skirting may be mitred, as above, or coped, where one length of timber runs straight into the corner. The other length of timber is then cut to carefully mould around the contours of the first piece. In all cases, joints should be flush, tight and neatly finished.

Finish - The finished surface of skirting and architrave may be either painted or varnished wood. In either case, the wood should have been well sanded, presenting a smooth finish.
Nail and screw holes, and any indentations caused by knots, should be filled and sanded and not be visible after painting.

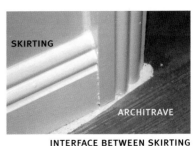

INTERFACE BETWEEN SKIRTING
AND ARCHITRAVE

At the interface between skirting/architrave and the wall, a bead of mastic should close any gaps. Gaps should, however, not be more than 3mm at any point.

Level - Where skirting meets the floor, a consistent, small gap should be apparent. If the gap is greater than about five milimetres, skirting was poorly applied and should be redone. If gaps are only present in some places, the floor may not be level (see Floors p.28).

The edge of the architrave closest to the doorframe should be set away from the doorframe by about five milimetres, and this distance should be consistent around the entire frame.

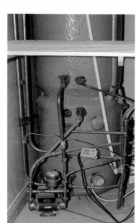

HOT PRESS

HOT PRESS

The hot press may or may not be painted. Check your specification or show unit. All vertical pipes going into the attic should be clipped neatly to the wall.

All electrical cables should be tidy and secure.

Spar or slatted shelving should be provided above the cylinder.

All holes in the floor, walls and ceiling where pipes penetrate should be filled.

The hot press area should be free of debris.

HOT PRESS

BATHROOM

LOOK FOR
BATH AND SANITARY WARE / SEALS / BATH AND SHOWER SCREEN / VENTILATION

TAKE ACTION

Bath and Sanitary Ware - The bath is usually made of plastic. Some baths may be made of cast iron.

TAP AND SEAL BETWEEN BATH AND TILES

All sanitary ware should be checked for scratches or chips. Where the toilet is screwed to the ground, hairline cracks can appear on the ceramic surrounding the base and are easy to miss. So look carefully.

Seals - The gap where the bath meets the adjacent wall must be sealed. This can be done with a silicone seal or with a rubber tile trim. Both are effective. Ensure that there are no gaps. Where the bath meets the wall, press down firmly with your hand. It should not move. The bath has least support on either side of the taps. Be especially careful to check for unwanted movement there.

SHOWER SCREEN

Bath and Shower Screens - If bath and shower screens are supplied by the builder, turn on the shower hose and point it at the glass door to check for leaks. Do not do a DIY installation on bath and shower screens as incorrect installation frequently causes leaks. Get them installed by a professional.

Ventilation - If the bathroom does not have a window, mechanical ventilation must be supplied. (See Ventilation p.36)

"The first thing you should do
on entering your property to do your
snag list is turn on the heating"

PLUMBING

LOOK FOR
HEATING / LEAKS /
FITTINGS AND CONNECTIONS

TAKE ACTION

Heating - The first thing you should do when you enter your property to do your snag list is turn on the heating. It will take about thirty minutes for the heat to reach its maximum. Check that all radiators are working. Make sure to turn off heating when finished.

Leaks - Leaks from radiators are most likely to occur when the system is cooling down and the fittings contract, so check under each radiator. Turn on all taps in kitchen, bathroom, en suite, showers, etc. Let them run for about five minutes while you check them intermittently for leaks. Check in the hot press, under sinks, boiler and bath if accessible.

One at a time, put the stopper into each sink and bath allowing the water to spill into the overflow. Again, check underneath for leaks.

Fittings and Connections - All pipes feeding into radiators should be neatly finished. Where the pipe is straight, it should enter the radiator at either 90 degrees or 180 degrees. If an angle occurs along the length of the visible pipe, it should be a right angle and should be neatly finished.

Pipes may either be painted or not. They should not, however, be painted on the room side only. If unpainted, there should be no paint splashes.

Under the kitchen sink, located at the back of the unit, is a mains stopcock for water. This should be easily accessible for turning on and off. All taps should be securely fitted.

PIPE TO RADIATOR

**INCORRECT
ALIGNMENT OF
PIPE TO RADIATOR**

STOPCOCK UNDER SINK

"The Electricity Supply Board

(ESB) requires a detailed certificate from the builder. It should be signed by a licensed registered electrical contractor (RECI/AECI/ECSSA)"

ELECTRICS

Strict safeguards are in place to ensure that electric systems meet minimum standards on all new building developments.

The Electricity Supply Board (ESB) requires a detailed certificate from the builder. It should be signed by a licensed registered electrician (RECI - Register of Electrical Contractors of Ireland / AECI - Association of Electrical Contractors of Ireland / ECSSA - Electrical Contractors Safety and Standards Association). You may request this through your solicitor.

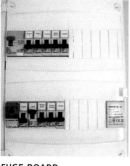

FUSE BOARD

Electricity supply will not be switched on until all requirements are satisfied. Therefore, snagging of electrics deals with cosmetic items only.

LOOK FOR
FUSE BOARD / SOCKETS, SWITCHES / LIGHTS

TAKE ACTION
Fuse board - The fuse board must be clearly visible and easily accessible. Each breaker on the fuse board should be clearly labelled, indicating which circuit it serves.

LIGHT SWITCH

Sockets, Switches - Sockets and light switches should be clean, neatly installed, and level. Check that the number of sockets and light switches in each room is as shown in the show house, or in your contract. Plug in a hairdryer to check the socket function.

Lights - To snag the lights, it is advisable to bring your own 60W bulb. This is for two reasons. The first is to check that each light fixture is working. The second is to more clearly show up defective paintwork, plastering, etc.

POSITIONING ROSETTE FOR LIGHT PENDANT

The circular part of a light which attaches to the ceiling is called the rosette. The part which hangs down is the pendant. The rosette is sometimes partially detached for painting. If it is still detached, instruct the builder to reattach it.

PAINTWORK

Paintwork defects are the most common items appearing on snag lists. Because there may be several different paintwork items in one room, try to be as specific as possible in describing the location of each paint problem - e.g. one metre left of window. It is important to get the paint finish right as this is one of the hallmarks of excellence in the finished product.

ROUGH INCONSISTENT PAINTWORK

LOOK FOR
PREPARATION / FINISH / INTERFACES

TAKE ACTION

Preparation - Check that wall surfaces are flat and smooth. Irregular patterned lines on the surface of the wall can indicate poor plasterwork which should have been addressed prior to painting. Poor plasterwork should be corrected if present.

Where walls have been damaged due to inserting sockets, etc, repairs should not be visible under the paintwork.

Finish - Paintwork should be smooth and consistent. Brush marks should not be visible. Colour finish should be even. Surrounding surfaces should be free of paint splashes.

POORLY FINISHED PAINTWORK

Interfaces - Where there is a transition between paint colours, as where a wall meets a ceiling or door architrave, the line should be neatly finished and straight.

TILING

LOOK FOR
CONTRACT / JOINTS / CUTS / GROUTING

TAKE ACTION

Contract - The amount of tiling provided by a given builder / developer differs. Check your contract to ensure that the builder has tiled all areas specified in the contract. If your development has a show house, remember that the actual tiles provided to you may differ because of availability. However, the replacement tiles should be similar or of greater value.

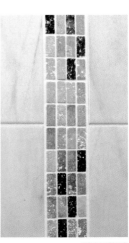

GROUTING

Joints - Tiles should be aligned in straight lines. All gaps should be even. The overall surface should be smooth and flat.

Cuts - Where tiles have had to be cut, for example to fit around sockets or toilets, the cuts should be done neatly and evenly. Ensure that there are no broken tiles.

Grouting - The spaces between tiles are filled with grout. It should be neatly applied and have a consistent texture and finish - no bumps or hollows. There should be no grout on the surface of the tiles.

VENTILATION

INSIDE LOUVRED VENT

LOOK FOR
ROOM VENTILATION / MECHINICAL VENTILATION / ATTIC VENTILATION

TAKE ACTION
Room ventilation - Each habitable room must have external ventilation. This is usually achieved by an opening in an external wall or window or both. Ventilation through a wall is provided by a cylindrical opening that is covered by an interior plastic grill.

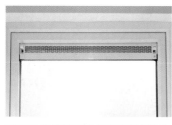

INSIDE ADJUSTABLE WINDOW VENT

Look through the grill (at an angle, as the grill is louvred), to ensure that the opening has not become blocked with debris during the building process.

A window vent is a grill located at the top of the glass. It has a handle allowing the grill to be opened and closed. Ensure that it is in working order.

It is essential that rooms are adequately ventilated. See Definitions p.60 for some considerations that may arise in the absence of appropriate ventilation.

MECHANICAL VENT IN BATHROOM

Mechanical ventilation - Kitchens and bathrooms that don't have windows require mechanical ventilation in addition to external ventilation as described above. An electric fan extracts moisture and fumes from the room through ducting which exits through the roof or otherwise externally. The fan is typically wired through the lightswitch: when the light is on you should hear the fan running. When the light is switched off the fan will continue to run for about three minutes.

To check that the fan is extracting, hold a light piece of paper against it. The paper should be pulled against the grill.

Attic ventilation - The attic is ventilated to equalise air pressure during windy weather and also to preserve attic timbers. Check that the insulation, which is placed between joists, stops at the point where the joists meet the rafters. If it is packed out into the angle between the roof and the attic floor, it may prevent proper ventilation.

FLEXIBLE DUCTING TO VENTILATION IN ATTIC

Bathroom or kitchen extractor fans and ventilation waste pipes from toilets are sometimes run through the attic. A flexible tube will be seen extending from the bottom of the attic to a vented tile or slate. Ensure that the pipe is securely fastened and sealed at both ends, and that there is a gradual fall with no kinks or curves in the pipe.

FIRE PREVENTION

LOOK FOR
FIRE ALARMS

TAKE ACTION
Every property should be fitted with a smoke and a heat alarm. These are wired directly to the main power and also have battery backup. In order to conserve battery power, it may not be connected until the owner moves in. If the battery is not connected or if the battery power is low, the unit will emit regular beeping sounds.

SMOKE DETECTOR

In apartment blocks, fire detectors are also wired to a fire panel which is usually located in the main lobby to assist in the location of fires. A copy of the fire safety certificate may be requested from your solicitor.

BUILT-IN UNITS

Snagging for built-in units such as wardrobes is identical to that for kitchen presses.

Exterior Snagging

With the Universal Snag List in hand, start on the outside of the house or apartment and work clockwise where possible.

Start at say the front door and work around the house or apartment back to the front door and tell the builder that you have done so. By following your sequence, the builder will be better able to check your findings systematically to discover what may have been overlooked.

For Exterior Snagging, inspect the roof, chimney, brickwork, plastering, windows, exterior doors, balcony, foundations, landscaping, fencing, driveways and services.

ROOF
Type of Roof

Flat Roof - This is usually made of felt, asphalt, green mineral or galvanised sheeting. Check that it does not hold water and that all water flows down the roof to the drains.

Pitched Roof - This is usually constructed of tile or slate. Look for any broken tiles or slates. The filling between ridge tiles is called pointing. This should be neatly finished and should match the colour of the tiles.

LOOK FOR
TYPE OF ROOF / DEBRIS / ROOF VENTS /
FASCIA BOARD / SOFFIT / GUTTER / DOWNPIPE

TAKE ACTION

Debris - Stand well back from the house and survey the roof. If you see debris such as pieces of mortar or tile on the roof, ask the builder to remove it and clean the roof.

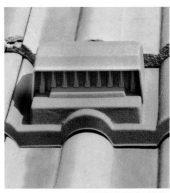

TILED ROOF VENT

Roof vents - Roof vents are pipes through which odours and steam from kitchen, bathroom and soil vents are expelled. Check that each roof vent has a corresponding pipe inside the attic, apart from one dedicated attic vent.

Fascia board - This is a flat board, made of wood, PVC or aluminum which covers the ends of rafters on the exterior of a roof. Where lengths of fascia board meet, 'joiners' should be used to bridge the joint.

Soffit - This is the undersurface of overhanging eaves constructed of wood or PVC with vents. The vents described in the section on snagging the attic space (see page 37) will be visible on the exterior soffits at approximately two metre intervals.

Gutter - Water in the gutter needs to flow towards the down-pipe. However, if insufficient brackets have been installed, there may be a curve in the gutter. Check the adjacent wall for staining in the area of joints, as this may indicate leaking. Ask the builder to cut off any excess felt over the gutter as wind may cause it to vibrate noisily.

Down-pipe - Ensure that down-pipes are vertical - if not, this will usually be evident at a short distance and may be confirmed with a spirit level. At least three wall brackets should be used on a typical two-storey house. Ensure that the down-pipe outlet discharges directly into the drain.

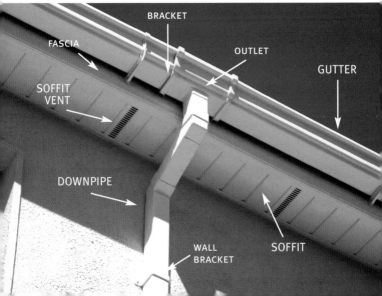

CROW STOPPERS

CHIMNEY POTS

CAPPING

POINTING

BRICK WORK

LEAD FLASHING

CHIMNEY

LOOK FOR
LEAD FLASHING / POINTING / CHIMNEY POT (FLUE) /
CROW - STOPPER / DEBRIS / DRAG

TAKE ACTION
Lead Flashing - Lead flashing prevents rainwater from getting through
where the chimney meets the roof. Flashing comprises multiple sheets of
lead (usually grey-black in colour) placed neatly around the base of the
chimney and spread out over the junction with the roof in a short skirt.
Check that the lead flashing overlaps the junction completely and neatly.

Pointing - Check that the pointing (mortar filled gaps) between the bricks
in the chimney walls is clean, neat and tidy.

Chimney Pot (Flue) - Check that the chimney pot, a clay pipe, often
terracotta in colour, which extends above the brickwork in the chimney, is
not cracked. You should be able to see the chimney pot from the ground
by standing back some distance.

Crow - stopper - It is a good idea for chimneys to be fitted with crow stoppers (usually wire cages), to prevent crows and other birds from nesting. Some builders provide them. If not, plan to have them installed after you take ownership of the property.

Debris - Go into the house or apartment and, from inside the fireplace, look up the chimney to check that it is free of debris such as falling plaster or bird-nests which may be lodged there.

Drag - Ask the builder to ensure that the chimney is clear. Then, as soon as the property becomes yours, make sure that the chimney has a drag. Light a fire to make sure that the smoke goes up the chimney and not into the room. If it goes into the room, advise the builder.

BRICKWORK

LOOK FOR
POINTING / BRICKWORK / BRICK VENTS / MORTAR SPLASHES / EFFLORESCENCE

TAKE ACTION
Pointing - The mortar in between the bricks should be neat and tidy. If not, ask the builder to rake out joints and re-point it.

EFFLORESENCE ON BRICKWORK

Brickwork - Cracked bricks should be replaced. Uneven brickwork should be rectified. All gaps between windows, doors and exterior finish should be sealed.

Brick Vents - Each interior room vent should correspond to a vent on the external wall. Brick vents are usually plastic and look like a louvered brick. To snag, ensure that its surface is undamaged and free of mortar splashes.

Mortar splashes - If there is excess mortar, or splashes of mortar on brickwork, the brickwork should be scraped off and cleaned.

Efflorescence - This white deposit on brickwork can only be rectified by time. See Definitions p.60.

PLASTERING

LOOK FOR
CHIPS / CRACKS / FLASHING / ROUGH FINISH / UNEVEN SURFACE / PLASTER VENTS

TAKE ACTION
Chips - Chips in the plaster should be filled in and painted

Cracks - Minor hairline cracks are caused by the drying-out process and are common. These can be raked out and re-plastered but may recur. More extensive cracks could indicate structural problems. Bring this to the attention of your builder, but, if in doubt, seek independent professional advice.

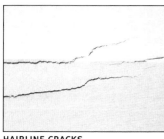
HAIRLINE CRACKS

Flashing - Where hairline cracks appear on plaster due to failure to bond, tap the plaster to ascertain if there is a hollow sound known as flashing. If hollow, the plaster should be removed and the wall re-plastered.

Rough Finish - If the wall has a rough finish, it should be rectified by re-plastering if necessary.

Uneven Surface - If plastered surface exhibits humps and hollows, your builder may plaster over the existing finish or remove the plaster and re-apply it.

Plaster Vents - See Brick Vents p.41: On plastering however, usually a metal louvered plate will correspond with the internal vent. Check that the nails which held the vent in place during plastering have been removed. Check that the vent is undamaged and that slits are not clogged with plaster.

WINDOWS

Windows may be PVC, timber, softwood or hardwood. Each type of window can present similar problems.

LOOK FOR
CHIPS ON FRAME / SCRAPES ON FRAME / HINGES / WEEP HOLES / SCRATCHES ON GLASS / RUBBER GASKET /SILICONE SEAL / WINDOW SILL

DAMAGED WINDOW FRAME

TAKE ACTION

Chips on frame - Most minor chips on PVC and timber windows can be patched. Note them on your snag list.

Scrapes on frame - Most scrapes on window frames can be sanded and filled easily.

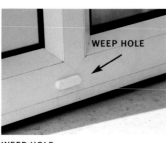
WEEP HOLE

Hinges - Check that the main window opens ninety degrees and closes with ease. Make sure that the track on the bottom of the window frame is clean and clear of debris.

Weep holes - Weep holes are located at the base of the window frame. On PVC frames ensure that there are caps over these holes. On timber frames, check that holes are present.

Scratches on glass - Stand two metres back from the glass and check glass for scratches. Do this in sunlight if possible.

Rubber gasket - This is the seal that weatherproofs between the glass and frame. Check that it is continuous, even, and evenly jointed.

Silicone seal - This is the seal between the frame and brickwork. It should be neatly applied, and have no gaps. The silicone strip should be no wider than 12 mm.

SILICONE SEAL

Window sill - This may be timber, PVC, aluminium, brick, or most commonly pre-cast concrete. For PVC, follow instructions above for PVC window frame. For brick, see Brickwork on page 41. Concrete sills are prone to being cracked or chipped during construction. They can be patched, or, in severe cases replaced.

EXTERIOR DOORS

LOOK FOR
DENTS AND SCRAPES / LEVEL / RUBBER GASKET / SILICONE SEAL

TAKE ACTION
Dents and scrapes - Check thoroughly all around the door and the doorframe. The bottom and side of the doorframe in particular may have accumulated dents and scrapes. The reason is that tools and materials are dragged through the doorway during the building phase causing inevitable damage. Minor damage can be repaired. But if it is severe the door may need to be replaced.

TYPICAL FRONT DOOR

Level - See Interior Doors p.29.

Rubber gasket - This is a rubber strip on the doorframe, facing the door. With door closed, check all around the perimeter of the door and in particular on the bottom of the doorframe, as this may have been damaged or removed during construction.

Silicone seal - This is the seal between the frame and brickwork. It should be neatly applied with no gaps. The silicone strip should be no wider than twelve millimetres.

BALCONY

A balcony may be flat roofed, have paving and walls, metal railings, decking etc.

LOOK FOR
METAL WORK / WALL / FLOOR

BALCONY

TAKE ACTION
Metal work - Shake the railings to make sure that they are secure. Check that gaps in rails are no more than 100 mm apart.

Wall - If a balcony has walls, snag as for exterior walls. Check that the capping (the stone on the top of the wall) is secure.

Floor - If there is floor paving, check that there is a gentle slope outwards for drainage. If there is decking, make sure that it is securely fixed to prevent warping of boards.

FOUNDATIONS

Foundations in general are difficult for the lay person to assess but potential problems may be suggested by cracks in walls, mostly exterior walls, running from the ground upwards.

If you suspect problems with the foundations, inform your builder immediately. Follow up by contacting your structural guarantor, for example HomeBond / Premier, who will liaise with the builder to ensure that appropriate action is taken.

If you do not have a ten year structural guarantee, contact your builder anyway. Most builders will be anxious to preserve their good name.

DIGGING FOUNDATIONS

LANDSCAPING

Note: Apartment complexes will usually be surrounded by exterior landscaped areas, and snagging of these areas is usually not required of the individual apartment purchasers. The management company is responsible for snagging in this situation.

LOOK FOR
DEBRIS / EVEN SURFACE / DRAINAGE / PLANTING

TAKE ACTION
Debris - Check through loose soil, or grass/planted areas for building debris. Check in particular for yellow or red plastic ties (bindings) discarded from bales of blocks. These can be embedded in the soil. Ask your builder to tidy and remove the ties.

Even surface - Ensure that there are no lumps or hollows in the garden. If the garden slopes towards the property, ask the builder to ensure that water does not flow onto the path surrounding the house.

LANDSCAPING

Drainage - Walk through loose soil, or grass/planted areas. Ensure that there is no lodging of water on the surface. If the weather has been dry, but water has lodged previously, the surface of the soil will be smooth.

This will be visible even through grass. Ask your builder to ensure that the soil is adequately drained.

Planting - Where planting has been included as part of the landscaping, check that, based on your contract, the correct amount has been provided. Some builders will sow grass seeds and provide plants. Others will just level the soil.

The show house will provide a good indication of what to expect in terms of quantity, although expect variations in the actual plants provided. The season will dictate what is suitable for planting at a particular time. Check that plants are healthy. If not, ask the builder to replace them.

"The correct location of your boundary is of great importance and has legal standing"

FENCING

LOOK FOR
BOUNDARY LOCATION / TYPE OF FENCING / STABILITY OF FENCING / ALIGNMENT / FINISH

TAKE ACTION
Boundary location - The correct location of your boundary is of great importance and has legal standing. It will have been clearly established as part of planning permission, and will be specified on your contract drawings. If you have not been furnished with these, request them through your solicitor. Measure all distances as indicated on the drawings to ensure that they tally.

CONCRETE AND TIMBER PANELLED FENCING

Type of fencing - Check what type of fencing was specified in your contract.

Stability of fencing - Where fencing is timber, or concrete post, walk along fence and shake it at several points. There should be minimal movement. Fencing will have "support posts" at intervals. These posts are usually embedded in concrete to ensure stability. Ensure that this concrete does not protrude above the level of the surrounding soil.

Alignment - Stand and look along the length of the fencing. It should be straight. Individual posts should be vertical.

Finish - Boundary fencing can sometimes be damaged during the landscaping process. Check that fencing is not chipped, damaged, or dirty.

"Individual cobbles should be
evenly laid, and joints between cobbles should be filled with dry cobble sand"

DRIVEWAYS

Driveways commonly consist of cobblelock, tarmac/asphalt, concrete/brick effect concrete or pea gravel.

LOOK FOR
SURFACE FINISH / DRAINAGE

COBBLELOCK DRIVEWAY

TAKE ACTION
Surface finish - For cobblelock driveways, check that the outer edge of cobblelock is held in place (benched) with a line of concrete. To check this, scrape back any soil at edge of cobblelock and the concrete will be visible. Individual cobbles should be evenly laid, and joints between cobbles should be filled with dry cobble sand. No open joints should be visible. There should be no broken edges or stains on cobbles.

Tarmac or asphalt surfaces should be laid evenly without dips or hollows. An edge of brick or treated timber should be present at interface with soil.

For concrete, or brick effect concrete, check the surface for overall evenness. However, the surface should not be overly smooth as it may present a slipping hazard. No stones or air holes should be apparent.

Pea gravel comes in many different sizes and colours. The important issue is the base provided for the pea gravel which is usually built of compressed stone. This means that stones of about thirty to forty millimetres in diameter, have been pounded with sand into a solid flat surface. Scrape back the pebbles to reveal this base. Pea gravel should be retained at the sides of the driveway by edging. Various types of edging, cobblelock or concrete for example, are available. The edging prevents migration or movement of pea gravel.

DRAIN CHANNEL

Drainage - Generally the driveway should have an even surface and slope away from the building to carry rainwater to the drain. In certain circumstances, e.g. hilly locations, the driveway will slope in towards the house. In this situation a gully, or grill should be provided.

DRAINAGE AT DOOR

"For ESB or Gas box, *snagging is limited to checking for splashes of concrete on the boxes and chips and scrapes*"

SERVICES
LOOK FOR
ESB BOX / GAS BOX OR OIL TANK / EIRCOM AND N.T.L. EXTERNAL TERMINATING UNITS (E.T.U) / WATER STOPCOCK

TAKE ACTION
ESB box -The electricity meter, or ESB box, (visible as a white plastic box with a door) is, in most cases, located on a gable wall near the front door. To open it, use the triangular key supplied by the builder. Good hardware stores sell this key also.

ESB METER BOX

Check the meter when you take possession of the property. Before the ESB turn on the supply, they will have confirmed that the box is installed in compliance with their regulations.

Snagging is limited to checking for splashes of concrete on the box and chips and scrapes. Ensure that there is a continuous seal of silicone on the perimeter of the box if it is built in to a brick wall.

In an apartment block, the meter is usually located in the central lobby, although this may vary. You should check with your builder. The meter would not form part of the snag list for an apartment.

GAS METER BOX

Gas box or Oil tank - The gas box is usually located beside the ESB box. Snagging is as for the ESB box. The gas company is responsible for checking that connections are up to standard. The box may be opened using the same key that accesses the ESB box. The meter should also be read when you sign over the house.

At any time, if the odour of gas is detected, call the gas company and leave the house/apartment. (See Useful Phone Numbers p.59.)

If your heating fuel is oil, the oil tank is usually located in the side or rear garden. Ensure that the block walls which support the oil tank are level and secure. The copper pipe (feed) from the tank to the boiler should be protected, usually with plastic, where it is above ground. If there is an external boiler house, its roof, walls, door, etc, should be snagged using the guidelines for the rest of the house. All cables and pipes should be installed neatly.

NTL

EIRCOM

ETU BOXES

Eircom and NTL ETU - The ETU boxes are usually located below/beside ESB and Gas boxes. These are small plastic boxes, either white or grey in colour. Again, check for chips and scrapes and splashes of concrete on the box. (see photo)

Water stopcock - This is located on the public footpath outside the property boundary. The cover should be easily visible, and accessible. With a screwdriver, the cover should be easily opened. Within, the square ended tap should be standing straight up and not bent to the side. The hole should be free of debris.

MAINS WATER
STOPCOCK CLOSED

MAINS WATER
STOPCOCK OPEN

GENERAL INDICATORS

Good indicators of a quality property development and good houses are cleanliness and completeness. The external clues will indicate the quality of internal care in building and presentation of the house or apartment.

Here is a checklist of the finishing touches that indicate a quality property:

Lawns	Are the lawns cut, clean, neat and tidy? Are the edges of lawns trimmed?
Landscaping	Are all shrubs, plants, flowers and bedding clean, neat and tidy?
Pathways	Are the pathways swept clean?
Windows	Are all window frames and glass clean?
Driveways	Are the driveways free of weeds and debris?
Rubbish	Have all building construction materials been removed? And have all rubbish skips been removed from the site?
Debris Free	Has all debris and dust been removed?
Roadways	Have all holes in the roadways been filled?

If any of these issues are outstanding, ask your builder to resolve them.

Good Questions

Can I close without a Snag List?
You are not legally obliged to submit a snag list. However, it is advisable to ensure that you are happy with your new home.

Can I do Snag List after closing?
No. However, if you uncover problems after closing, inform your builder. A reputable builder will address all reasonable requests.

How many Snag Lists can I submit? **Normally one.**

Can I snag my own house?
Yes. Snagging is considered to cover minor defects, cosmetics and function in the main and therefore can be undertaken by the layperson. When in doubt consult a professional.

Should the property be left clean for the surveyor/snagger?
This varies from builder to builder. Usually it is broom-cleaned for snagging and professionally cleaned for closing.

Who is responsible for dealing with problems such as popped nails and minor cracks after I close?
They will be dealt with if noted on your snag list. However, these items may recur later. After closing, it will be your responsibility to deal with them. See Technical Tips p.56.

Can I do any work on house before I close, e.g., install carpets, have furniture delivered etc? Usually not, but it varies from builder to builder.

What protection do I have if I discover problems after I close?
Structural problems will be covered by your 10 year guarantee. If applicable, discuss other problems with your builder and/or home owner's insurance company.

SPECIFIC QUESTIONS FOR YOUR BUILDER

What time period is allowed to complete a Snag List?

Can I make changes - if so, what are the implications?

What is included in my closing package?

Can I get direct phone numbers for sub contractors?

How do I transfer gas and electricity bills into my name?

"Structural problems will be covered by your 10 year guarantee."

Construction - If your new home is being built from scratch, ask the builder/developer how long the property will be under construction. If it is part of a larger development, how long will the estate, or apartment block be under construction?

Closing Date - Confirm with your builder/developer the estimated finishing date by which your house, duplex or apartment will be completed. Then allow at least one month after this date to allow for snagging. The solicitor will complete paperwork and draw down finance from your lending institution. The builder should tell you when your property is ready for snagging.

Picture Hanging - Before hanging pictures on your walls, ask the builder what are the best fixings to use for the particular wall type. Ask builder to guide you as to the locations of electric cables. As a general rule, all cables run vertically from the socket or light switch with a few exceptions which occur mainly if sockets are very close together.

SPECIFIC QUESTIONS FOR YOUR ESTATE AGENT

What is the floor area of my property?

How much is the annual maintenance fee for an apartment?
What does it include? What does it not include?

How many Telephone and T.V. points are included and where are they located? Check show units or drawings.

What size openings are left for kitchen appliances?
Usually 600 millimetres, but it is advisable to check.

Can I upgrade - e.g. kitchen units, appliances, tiles, fireplaces etc?

Do I get an extractor fan?

Do I get shower and bath screens?

SPECIFIC QUESTIONS FOR YOUR SOLICITOR

Where do I pick up my keys after I close?

Can I be supplied with documentation relating to issues such as boundary location, fire certification, electrical and gas certification.

Do I have a structural guarantee? If so, what does it cover?

New **House Tips**

SHOPS/SUPERMARKET/SCHOOLS - Walk to the shops / supermarkets / schools and then walk back to your new home laden down with shopping. Does it take more than ten minutes?

SCHOOLS - Check the distance of primary schools, secondary schools and colleges from your new home.

If you are a parent of a young child, consider that you may have to book a place in the school for your child four years in advance of the child starting school.

WORKPLACE DISTANCE AND COSTS - Check how far your workplace is from your new home. Consider the cost and time benefit of using public transport to get to and from work during rush hour.

PUBLIC TRANSPORT DISTANCE - Check the distance from your new home to public transport for example, the bus stop, the LUAS line, the train station.

AMENITIES AND FACILITIES - Check the location of amenities and facilities - church, sports facilities, parks, playgrounds, health clubs and pubs - in relation to each other and to your home. This has travel, cost, time and safety implications for entertainment, education and community involvement for parents and children.

PARKING - Check the availability of private and public parking and how much it might cost you per week. Consider how many cars are allowed in the parking area and check that it is secure.

THE LOCALS HAVE IT - If you are new to the area, go to the pub, talk to the local residents and read the local newspapers over a few weeks. Ask the right questions and you will learn from them things you might never have considered e.g. about the quality of public transport, services, attitude and culture of the locals, level of crime, presence of the Gardai and so on.

DELAYS - Good builders and developers will attempt to have your new house or apartment finished as quickly as possible. However, their best attempts may be delayed or hampered for a number of reasons. These reasons may include:

- Delays in electricity supply connection.

- Delays in gas supply connection.

- Delays in public lighting connection.

- Specialist staff such as bricklayers may be in short supply.

- Lack of availability of equipment such as cranes, or excavators.

- Adverse weather conditions which can delay any work for many weeks.

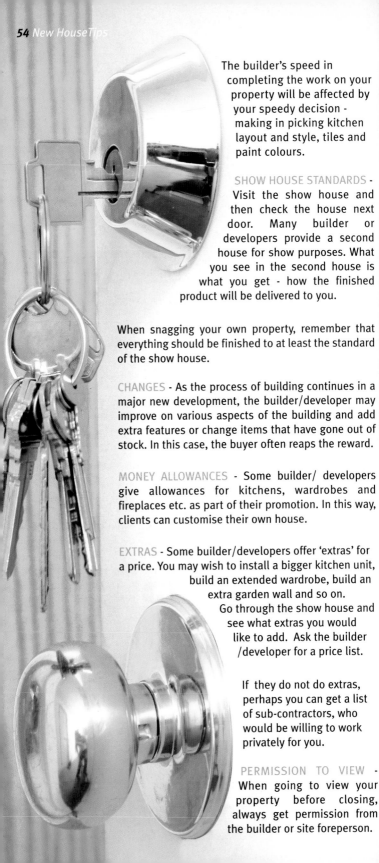

The builder's speed in completing the work on your property will be affected by your speedy decision - making in picking kitchen layout and style, tiles and paint colours.

SHOW HOUSE STANDARDS - Visit the show house and then check the house next door. Many builder or developers provide a second house for show purposes. What you see in the second house is what you get - how the finished product will be delivered to you.

When snagging your own property, remember that everything should be finished to at least the standard of the show house.

CHANGES - As the process of building continues in a major new development, the builder/developer may improve on various aspects of the building and add extra features or change items that have gone out of stock. In this case, the buyer often reaps the reward.

MONEY ALLOWANCES - Some builder/ developers give allowances for kitchens, wardrobes and fireplaces etc. as part of their promotion. In this way, clients can customise their own house.

EXTRAS - Some builder/developers offer 'extras' for a price. You may wish to install a bigger kitchen unit, build an extended wardrobe, build an extra garden wall and so on. Go through the show house and see what extras you would like to add. Ask the builder /developer for a price list.

If they do not do extras, perhaps you can get a list of sub-contractors, who would be willing to work privately for you.

PERMISSION TO VIEW - When going to view your property before closing, always get permission from the builder or site foreperson.

STRUCTURAL GUARANTEE - Check that your builder/developer is registered with Homebond or Premier or similar association who provide a ten year structural guarantee.

DRYING OUT - When moving into a new property, open windows and have heat on low so as to let it dry slowly and acclimatise. Always remember that, although insulation is necessary to conserve energy, it is essential that adequate ventilation is also provided.

MANAGEMENT COMPANIES - If your new apartment is part of a block, a complex or estate in which roads, gardens, entrances, stairwells, lifts, car parks, waste management and security and so on are shared in common, it makes good sense for the owners to employ a management company to manage and maintain these facilities for everybody.

A management company is usually employed initially by the builder/developer. Annual fees for the management company are outlined at the contract stage. It is important that you budget for this outlay.

When the builder/developer has completed work to the satisfaction of the residents and the management company, the development is signed over. Following this signing, the management company is then under contract to the owners.

The owners can terminate the contract of the management company and employ another if desired. Owners should engage with the management company in ongoing negotiations about management fees and level of service.

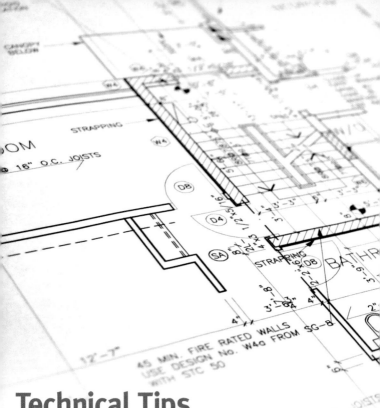

Technical Tips

WIRING PLANNING - When your electrician is doing the original wiring get extra wiring for your special music system speakers, television/computer in each bedroom, and your CCTV security system. This extra investment can save you lots of heartache, ripping up of floorboards, ceilings, attics, re-decoration and money later on.

GLASS SCRATCHES - To check glass for scratches and faults, stand two metres back inside and outside.

DRYING - It takes at least a year for materials such as timber and plaster used in the construction of your property to acclimatise. For this reason it is wise to allow this period of time to elapse before tackling the inevitable appearance of popped nails and hairline plaster cracks.

PLASTER CRACKS - Using the edge of a filling knife, rake out the plaster surrounding the crack in a 'V' shape. Fill with commercially available filler and allow to dry. Sand with fine sandpaper and then paint. Such cracks are common and may recur.

POPPED NAIL - To prevent a popped nail recurring, insert a screw about three centimeters vertically above or below the offending nail. Then, as above, fill the area, sand it and paint over.

WOODEN FLOORS AND MOISTURE READING - If you plan to install a wooden floor over a concrete floor, it is necessary to check the moisture content of the floor with a moisture content reader. This tool may be hired from a hire company. Alternatively, if a contractor is installing your floor, this should be provided as part of the service.

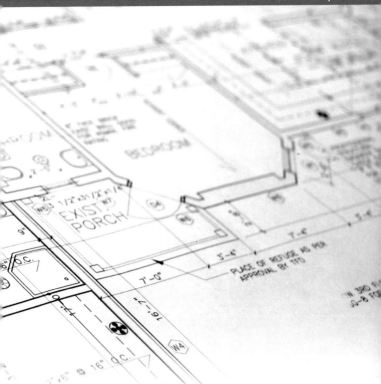

Follow manufacturer's guidelines as to the maximum moisture content permitted for a particular floor. If the moisture content is too high, postpone the job.

In any case, insist that a damp proof membrane be laid under the wooden floor. A gap of approximately ten millimetres must be left around the perimeter of the floor to allow for expansion of wood.

It is advised that the timber be left in the appropiate rooms in open packages, to acclimatise to the conditions for at least one week prior to laying.

SKIRTING BOARDS - When it is planned to install a wooden floor after closing, independent flooring contractors frequently advise buyers to have skirting tacked loosely rather than securely fastened by the builder. This is so it can be easily removed with minimal damage at the time of floor laying. Most builders will accommodate this request if it is made in time. However, the client should be aware that joints will not be as tightly finished in this situation. Check with your flooring contractor that final reinstallation of skirting is covered in their estimate.

RADIATORS - If a radiator is not heating, or is only partially heating, it probably has to be 'bled' which is the release of trapped air. To do so, turn on heating, get a vent key - (available in all hardware stores) - and locate the nut behind a top corner of the radiator. Hold kitchen paper underneath the nut to soak up water (the water will be dirty). Open it half way and air will come out. When water starts to come out with no air, then close the nut.

LEAKS - In the event of a leak, turn off the main stopcock located under your kitchen sink. Then proceed to the hot press and turn off all valves. If water is coming through your ceiling, puncture the ceiling with the handle of a floor brush. If you do not do this, the water force could cause the whole ceiling to collapse. This action will minimise damage while you contact a plumber to repair the fault.

DOMESTIC REFUSE - It is always a good idea to order your domestic refuse bins from your local authority a few weeks before you close to give them time to deliver. Remember you will have a lot of boxes and rubbish to get rid of when you move in.

READ ALL CONTRACTS CAREFULLY - Check your contract carefully. If there is anything you don't understand ask your solicitor.

USEFUL PHONE NUMBERS

BUILDER

FINISHING FOREPERSON

PLUMBER

CARPENTER

ELECTRICIAN

HANDYMAN

TILER

HEATING APPLIANCE SERVICE AGENT

REMOVALS COMPANY

LOCAL AUTHORITY

PLANNING

DOMESTIC REFUSE

NON-DOMESTIC REFUSE

ENVIRONMENT

MANAGEMENT COMPANY

BANK

BUILDING SOCIETY

CREDIT UNION

ESTATE AGENT

SOLICITOR

HOMEBOND

GARDAI, AMBULANCE, FIRE SERVICE   999 OR 112

GARDA CONFIDENTIAL LINE   1800 666 111

LOCAL GARDA STATION

ESB EMERGENCY

GAS (BORD GAIS) EMERGENCY   1850 20 50 50

DOCTOR

HOSPITAL

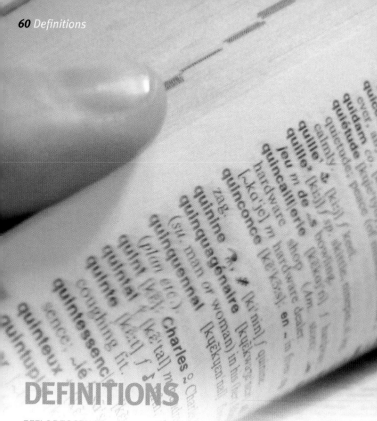

DEFINITIONS

EFFLORESCENCE

This appears as white powder on brick. Many clay bricks contain salts (sulphates). These salts may crystallise at the surface and give a white powder effect called efflorescence. Efflorescence is most noticeable during dry weather, which draws the salts out, and is usually harmless. Time, frost and exposure to the elements is the cure. It can be unsightly but will disappear over time.

TIMBER

Timber is an organic material widely used in the construction industry. Softwood timber (for example scots pine, Baltic redwood, Norway spruce, Baltic whitewood, larch, Douglas fir) is most commonly used. Because timber is organic, it is vulnerable to the elements and it may expand and contract when it takes in or loses moisture. This can explain why doors can become 'sticky' or loose in the early stages.

MOISTURE AND CONDENSATION

The construction industry has made strides in recent years in sealing up houses and apartments using double glazing, high density insulation, and so on. Rooms require ventilation however. They are ventilated using a vent on the wall or window. In addition to ventilation, all rooms need to be adequately heated.

Many homeowners/tenants block the vent during cold or windy weather. Due to the lack of ventilation, a musty smell may be noticed,

MOULD

followed by the appearance of a black mould behind a bedside locker, bed, or inside a wardrobe, where there is little circulation of air. This is caused by condensation.

THE TYPICAL DAILY MOISTURE PRODUCTION IN A HOUSEHOLD OF 5 PERSONS IS:

Activity	Moisture Emission (litres)
Clothes drying	5.0
Cooking	3.0
Paraffin heater	1.7
Two persons active for 16 hours	1.7
5 persons asleep for 8 hours	1.5
Bathing, dishwashing	1.0
Clothes washing	0.5
Total	14.4 litres

Just by normal breathing, one person produces at least 0.3 litres of moisture a day. General domestic activities can greatly increase this amount.

WATER DURING CONSTRUCTION

For brickwork alone in a typical house, as much as one tonne of water can be used. Much of this water evaporates before the house is completed. However it will take at least a year of heating and adequate ventilation for the house to dry out. Ventilation is the key element to remove tonnes of water that have built up during construction.

The Irish Home Buyer's Guide to Snagging

Use the specially designed Universal Snag List following to guide you towards creating your own snag list. Write the snags in a notepad.

Otherwise use the specially designed, downloadable, adjustable Universal Snag List on www.snagbook.com.

Simply then submit your completed Universal Snag list by hand, by post, by email, or by fax to your builder/developer and /or solicitor.

When the builder/developer returns to you and has indicated that snags on the snag list have been put into effect to your satisfaction, tick the 'completed' box.

UNIVERSAL
SNAG LIST

PROPERTY ADDRESS: _____

_____

_____

CLIENT NAME: _____

Address: _____

_____

_____

CONTACT DETAILS:

Work: _____

Home: _____

Mobile: _____

Email: _____

Fax: _____

SOLICITOR NAME:

Address: _____

_____

_____

CONTACT DETAILS:

Work: _____

Home: _____

Mobile: _____

Email: _____

Fax: _____

BUILDER NAME:

Address: _____

_____

_____

CONTACT DETAILS:

Work: _____

Home: _____

Mobile: _____

Email: _____

Fax: _____

FOREPERSON NAME:

Work: _____

COMPLET

KITCHEN

Walls: _____

Ceilings: _____

Skirting & Architrave: _____

Doors: _____

Floors: _____

Electrics: _____

Plumbing: _____

Painting: _____

Cleaning: _____

Windows: _____

Kitchen Units: _____

Appliances: _____

Tiling: _____

Ventilation: _____

COMPLETED

Vents: _____ ☐

_____

_____

ENTRANCE HALL

Walls: _____ ☐

_____

Ceilings: _____ ☐

_____

Skirting & Architrave: _____ ☐

_____

Doors: _____ ☐

_____

Floors: _____ ☐

_____

Stairs: _____ ☐

_____

Electrics: _____ ☐

_____

Plumbing: _____ ☐

_____

Painting: _____ ☐

_____

Cleaning: _____ ☐

_____

LIVING ROOM

Walls: _____ ☐

_____

Ceilings: _____ ☐

_____

_____

COMPLETE

Skirting & Architrave: _____ ☐

Doors: _____ ☐

Floors: _____ ☐

Stairs: _____ ☐

Electrics: _____ ☐

Plumbing: _____ ☐

Painting: _____ ☐

Cleaning: _____ ☐

Fireplace: _____ ☐

Windows: _____ ☐

Vents: _____ ☐

DINING ROOM

Walls: _____ ☐

Ceilings: _____ ☐

Skirting & Architrave: _____ ☐

COMPLETED

Doors: _____ [ ]

_____

Floors: _____ [ ]

_____

Electrics: _____ [ ]

_____

Plumbing: _____ [ ]

_____

Painting: _____ [ ]

_____

Cleaning: _____ [ ]

_____

Windows: _____ [ ]

_____

Vents: _____ [ ]

_____

UTILITY

Walls: _____ [ ]

_____

Ceilings: _____ [ ]

_____

Skirting & Architrave: _____ [ ]

_____

Doors: _____ [ ]

_____

Floors: _____ [ ]

_____

Electrics: _____ [ ]

_____

COMPLETE

Plumbing: _____ ☐

Painting: _____ ☐

Cleaning: _____ ☐

Windows: _____ ☐

Storage Units: _____ ☐

Appliances: _____ ☐

Boiler: _____ ☐

Vents: _____ ☐

Dryer Vent: _____ ☐

DOWNSTAIRS TOILET

Walls: _____ ☐

Ceilings: _____ ☐

Skirting & Architrave: _____ ☐

Doors: _____ ☐

Floors: _____ ☐

COMPLETED

Electrics: _____   ☐

_____

Plumbing: _____   ☐

_____

Painting: _____   ☐

_____

Cleaning: _____   ☐

_____

Windows: _____   ☐

_____

Ventilation: _____   ☐

_____

Sanitary Ware: _____   ☐

_____

Tiling: _____   ☐

_____

Extractor Fan: _____   ☐

_____

_____

UPSTAIRS LANDING

Walls: _____   ☐

_____

Ceilings: _____   ☐

_____

Skirting & Architrave: _____   ☐

_____

Doors: _____   ☐

_____

Floors: _____   ☐

_____

_____

_____

COMPLETE

Electrics: _____ ☐

Plumbing: _____ ☐

Painting: _____ ☐

Cleaning: _____ ☐

Windows: _____ ☐

Access Door: _____ ☐

Handrail: _____ ☐

BATHROOM

Walls: _____ ☐

Ceilings: _____ ☐

Skirting & Architrave: _____ ☐

Doors: _____ ☐

Floors: _____ ☐

Electrics: _____ ☐

Plumbing: _____ ☐

COMPLETED

Painting: _____ ☐

_____

Cleaning: _____ ☐

_____

Windows: _____ ☐

_____

Ventilation: _____ ☐

_____

Sanitary Ware: _____ ☐

_____

_____

Tiling: _____ ☐

_____

_____

MASTER BEDROOM

Walls: _____ ☐

_____

Ceilings: _____ ☐

_____

Skirting & Architrave: _____ ☐

_____

Doors: _____ ☐

_____

Floors: _____ ☐

_____

Electrics: _____ ☐

_____

Plumbing: _____ ☐

_____

Painting: _____ ☐

_____

COMPLETE

Cleaning: _____ ☐

Windows: _____ ☐

Ventilation: _____ ☐

Wardrobes: _____ ☐

ENSUITE

Walls: _____ ☐

Ceilings: _____ ☐

Skirting & Architrave: _____ ☐

Doors: _____ ☐

Floors: _____ ☐

Electrics: _____ ☐

Plumbing: _____ ☐

Painting: _____ ☐

Cleaning: _____ ☐

Windows: _____ ☐

COMPLETED

Ventilation: _____ ☐

_____

Sanitary Ware: _____ ☐

_____

Tiling: _____ ☐

_____

_____

HOT PRESS

Cylinder: _____ ☐

_____

Pipes: _____ ☐

_____

Shelving: _____ ☐

_____

Doors: _____ ☐

_____

Floors: _____ ☐

_____

Immersion: _____ ☐

_____

_____

BEDROOM 2

Walls: _____ ☐

_____

Ceilings: _____ ☐

_____

Skirting & Architrave: _____ ☐

_____

Doors: _____ ☐

_____

_____

COMPLETED

Floors: _____ ☐

Electrics: _____ ☐

Plumbing: _____ ☐

Painting: _____ ☐

Cleaning: _____ ☐

Windows: _____ ☐

Ventilation: _____ ☐

Wardrobes: _____ ☐

BEDROOM 3

Walls: _____ ☐

Ceilings: _____ ☐

Skirting & Architrave: _____ ☐

Doors: _____ ☐

Floors: _____ ☐

Electrics: _____ ☐

COMPLETED

Plumbing: _____ [ ]

_____

Painting: _____ [ ]

_____

Cleaning: _____ [ ]

_____

Windows: _____ [ ]

_____

Ventilation: _____ [ ]

_____

_____

Wardrobes: _____ [ ]

_____

_____

ATTIC

Access: _____ [ ]

_____

Insulation: _____ [ ]

_____

Ventilation: _____ [ ]

_____

Party wall (must reach underside of felt): _____ [ ]

_____

Cleaning: _____ [ ]

_____

Electrics: _____ [ ]

_____

Plumbing: _____ [ ]

_____

Tank Cover: _____ [ ]

_____

_____

EXTERIOR

COMPLETE

Roofs: _____ ☐

Chimneys: _____ ☐

Brickwork: _____ ☐

Plastering: _____ ☐

Windows: _____ ☐

Doors: _____ ☐

Balcony: _____ ☐

Landscaping: _____ ☐

Fencing: _____ ☐

Driveways: _____ ☐

Services: _____ ☐

UNIVERSAL SNAGLIST END NOTES

* Check all glass, sanitary ware and counters for scratches and replace as appropriate.

* Ensure that all scuffmarks on walls, ceilings and woodwork are touched up.

* Ensure that dwelling is in accordance with Building Regulations, including parts L and M.

* Ensure that all hinges and locks on doors and windows are in working order.

* No testing of plumbing, electrical items or drainage is presumed to have taken place for this report.

* No opening of walls, pipes, floors or roof has taken place for this report.

* This report, based only on a visual inspection, is not a structural survey. It is a snag list.

NOTES